PEACOCKS IN THE GLEN AGAIN

WITH ILLUSTRATIONS BY ROBBIE PETERSON

CAROLINE COPELAND

Copyright © 2016 Caroline Copeland

The moral right of the author has been asserted.

Apart from any fair dealing for the purposes of research or private study, or criticism or review, as permitted under the Copyright, Designs and Patents Act 1988, this publication may only be reproduced, stored or transmitted, in any form or by any means, with the prior permission in writing of the publishers, or in the case of reprographic reproduction in accordance with the terms of licences issued by the Copyright Licensing Agency. Enquiries concerning reproduction outside those terms should be sent to the publishers.

Matador
9 Priory Business Park,
Wistow Road, Kibworth Beauchamp,
Leicestershire. LE8 0RX
Tel: 0116 279 2299
Email: books@troubador.co.uk
Web: www.troubador.co.uk/matador
Twitter: @matadorbooks

ISBN 978 1785893 490

British Library Cataloguing in Publication Data.
A catalogue record for this book is available from the British Library.

Typeset in 14pt Chelsea Market by Troubador Publishing Ltd, Leicester, UK

Matador is an imprint of Troubador Publishing Ltd

Acknowledgements

A long history of philanthropy exists in Dunfermline, in most part thanks to the generosity of its most famous son, the millionaire philanthropist Andrew Carnegie, who was born and brought up in the town. However, generosity and kindness continue to flourish and it is thanks to that that this book exists.

Firstly, I would like to thank Cllr Neale Hanvey for supporting the project and introducing me to a group of people who have made the publication of Peacocks in the Glen Again possible.

These are:

Jim Stewart, Chair of Central Dunfermline Community Council, Treasurer Ben Evans, and all the amazingly positive members of that Community Council for their generous financial assistance and continued practical support.

Linsey Douglas from Fife Council, who has cheerfully helped with form-filling, advice, and a barrage of email correspondence.

The Fife Councillors who unanimously supported the project with a generous grant from Fife Council's Local Community Planning Budget.

The 10th Dunfermline Rainbows and their Leader, Elizabeth Fulton, for their kindness in fundraising for the project.

Pupils and Staff at Park Road Primary School, Rosyth for their input into the storyline: In particular, their Deputy Head Teacher Iona McDonald for inviting me into the school to speak to the children.

The Friends of Pittencrieff Park for their support, guidance and interest.

Visit Dunfermline for their kindness in marketing the book.

Lastly, and most importantly, I would like to thank the hugely talented artist Robbie Peterson of Dunfermline Art Club for his beautiful artwork. His evocative townscapes bring Dunfermline to life through the pages of this book. I am indebted to him for taking on this project and completing it so beautifully.

This book has very much been a community project and thanks to the help of the people and organisations named above, all profits from the sale of this book will go towards the care of the Peacocks in the Glen, and ensure their continuation in Pittencrieff Park, Dunfermline for many years to come.

Caroline Copeland
June 2016

Foreword

Peacocks have lived in Pittencrieff Park since 1905 when the Philanthropist Henry Beveridge returned to his hometown of Dunfermline from India, bringing with him the first Peacocks of Pittencrieff Park.

Known locally as The Glen, Pittencrieff Park was gifted to the townspeople of Dunfermline three years earlier in 1902, by Dunfermline's most famous son, Andrew Carnegie. Since then the majestic Peacocks have been given the Freedom of the City and are regularly seen strutting around the town and park.

For many years the birds thrived in Pittencrieff's seventy-five acres of parkland, but in recent times, the numbers of Peacocks living there has fallen… that is until recently, and the introduction of several new Peacocks and Peahens, and the arrival of one intrepid little Peacock called Andrew.

Peacocks in the Glen Again

Andrew Peacock had been listening to his mother's stories about her ancestral home for what seemed like forever. It had in fact only been a few months, but to Andrew who had the least attention span of any of the baby Peachicks, and more of an eye for adventure, it seemed like forever.

Mrs P would regularly gather her little Peachicks around her and tell them stories of the wonderful park with the rolling grassland, the waterfall, woodland, lily pond, bandstand and the lovely statue of Mr Carnegie. She told them that Pittencrieff Park had been home to her parents, her grandparents, her great grandparents, and even her great, great grandparents, for a very long time.

She would tell the Peachicks about the people who would come every day to feed them and how they would get into trouble from the Park Keeper who would tell them sternly "Not to Feed the Peacocks!" as he waved his finger and puffed his considerable sized chest out at them. Mrs P who loved her mid-morning snack, her afternoon snack, and her evening snack, was quite upset when she overheard the Park Keeper telling her visitors that the Peacocks had to be fed at regular times, and that because people insisted on feeding them ALL the time, some of the Peacocks were getting quite fat! Mrs P had never liked the Park Keeper anyway, but this made her furious with him.

She told the Peachicks that there had been Peacocks in Pittencrieff Park for over a hundred years. Andrew couldn't imagine how long one hundred years was, all he could think of was that it had been a long time since breakfast, and he was beginning to get very hungry.

When Mrs Peacock had been a young Peahen, her mother and father would gather her, and her brothers and sisters around and tell them stories about their proud heritage and how the Peacocks of Pittencrieff were the most honourable and noble of all the Scottish Peacocks. It was a matter of particular pride that the Pittencrieff Peacocks had lived in Mr Carnegie's Park for so many years, ever since Mr Beveridge had brought them from India.

Of course none of the existing Pittencrieff Peacocks had lived in India, but they had heard wonderful stories about it, and about how, when they arrived in Dunfermline and their beautiful new home, they were treated like royalty and given the Freedom of the City. Mrs P would ruffle her feathers and stick out her chest whenever she told this part of the story.

As a mark of respect to Andrew Carnegie, Mr and Mrs P would take their young Peachicks on a daily walk around the Park, through the Rose garden, and around Pittencrieff House, till they reached Mr Carnegie's statue. It was at this point that Mr P would pause in reverence to the great man and Mrs P would try to keep her little ones out of trouble.

Sometimes, depending on the weather – because Mrs P never liked to get her feathers too wet – they would venture out through the Louise Carnegie gates into the town where they would be admired by people out shopping or just going about their day.

The people of Dunfermline loved the Peacocks and would regularly stop and chat with them or try to feed them treats, but always out of sight of the Park Keeper, and much to Mrs Ps delight. At night the eerie scream of the Peacocks could often be heard in the darkened streets of the town. Once or twice, a particularly naughty Peacock would hide up one of the town's Closes and scream loudly at an unsuspecting passer-by or someone returning home late at night.

So many baby Peachicks were born that some of them went to live in other parts of Scotland. Mr and Mrs P were two of these "most special Peacocks" to move to Tullibole Castle near Kinross. Mrs P's friend Horatia Peahen could often be heard saying that Mrs P was so taken with the idea of living in a Castle that she couldn't wait to get to Tullibole. Mrs P had what Horatia called "ideas above her station" and was always quick to tell the other Peacocks and Peahens at Tullibole that she was in fact descended from the Peacocks of Pittencrieff Park.

Andrew Peachick had a sense of adventure that his brothers and sisters lacked. It was almost as if his mum's stories about their ancestral home in Pittencrieff Park had made them lazy and self satisfied. They were happy to strut around the grounds of Tullibole, and this was especially true whenever there was a wedding at the Castle.

People loved to get married at Tullibole Castle, and they really liked it when the Peacocks would strut around them when the photographs were being taken. Mischievous Andrew liked to peek out from behind the bride's dress just as the photographer took a photograph. Everyone would laugh – everyone that was apart from his mother who was

always "mortified" by his behaviour. Andrew didn't know what that meant, but his father told him that it was best not to ask.

Andrew was growing into a fine looking young Peacock. He was interested in the world outside of Tullibole Castle and liked nothing better than listening to the Gardeners and visitors talking about all of the things going on in the wide world. He heard people talking about exciting things going on in Andrew's ancestral home at Pittencrieff Park: events that had something to do with King Robert the Bruce who was the most famous King of Scotland, and who was now buried in Dunfermline Abbey.

Andrew thought of the stories he had heard about the Peacocks travelling from India and the adventures they must have had. He thought of all the exciting things that he'd heard visitors talk about as they strolled the gardens at Tullibole Castle: things he couldn't even imagine. Andrew knew that he wanted to see all the amazing things that he'd heard about.

As the vintage bus waited to take some wedding guests back to Dunfermline, Andrew hid behind the gateposts watching the guests climb onto the bus. He was a bit scared at first and wished that he was like other birds and could fly long distances high up in the sky. He had often thought that, especially when the ducks would tease him about not being able to fly like they could.

Once all the wedding guests, in their fancy hats, and top hats and tails were seated on the bus everyone began to cheer happily as the driver started to steer the bus out onto the road. Before Andrew knew what he was doing he had flown up onto the top of the old bus and perched himself

on the rail of one of the rear seats. He didn't feel scared at all when all the humans cheered again as they turned to look at him, and then just as quickly seemed to forget about him as they turned back to singing and clapping together. Andrew thought this was very strange behaviour.

From his vantage point high on the open top bus, Andrew could see all around him. He could see the Forth Rail Bridge and Forth Road Bridge stretch out over the River Forth, and then, over to his right, Andrew could see the tower of Dunfermline Abbey and the spires of the ancient town of Dunfermline rising around it, just as his mother had described it.

As the bus entered the High Street of Dunfermline, Andrew could see the turrets of the churches and the City Chambers, he saw people below looking up at him, shielding their eyes from the sun as the young Peacock sat proudly on top of the bus.

In front of him he could see large green parkland with lots of trees, and there, at the end of an avenue of trees, just as his mother had described it, was the large statue of Andrew Carnegie himself. Andrew swooped down from the bus, and landed on the gatepost.

Andrew felt alone and scared on his first night in the Park. He flew up into the high reaches of the trees and perched there just as his parents had shown him to. The park was quiet and there were no other Peacocks around to chat to. On that first night, little Andrew felt very alone and missed his family a lot. He was also beginning to feel hungry and realised that he hadn't eaten anything for some time.

As the sun began to rise over Pittencrieff Park, Andrew stretched and spread his beautiful tail feathers high up in his tree. For a moment he forgot where he was as he heard the screaming of other Peacocks in the distance. Suddenly, realising that he was no longer at home at Tullibole Castle, he flew down out of his tree and screamed back the familiar call of Peacocks into the early morning sunlight.

Slowly two or three Peacocks and Peahens made their way out of the bushes and trees towards where Andrew was strutting his feathers on the lawn.

Clive, the eldest of the Peacocks was the first to welcome Andrew to the park, and the two Peahens, Henrietta and Louise were very impressed with his beautiful plumage and handsome strutt as they all paraded around the Park showing Andrew the sights.

"Andrew", Clive said conspiratorially, "tomorrow, I will show you Dunfermline itself! We have, incase you didn't know, the Freedom of both the Park and the City."

Andrew who had heard so many stories about this from his mother, nodded in agreement with Clive. He felt very much at home here in Pittencrieff Park with his new friends and couldn't wait to see what this Freedom of Park and the City meant. Whatever it was, it had to be much more exciting than listening to his mother telling him to be home before sunset and listening to her interminable stories.

By the following Springtime, stories about Andrew's arrival in Pittencrieff Park and the new Peachicks that had been born, found their way back to Tullibole Castle and Mrs P.

Never had a Peahen felt so proud of her offspring. Here was another story to tell her new Peachicks and yet more evidence that the Peacocks of Pittencrieff Park really were the most splendid Peacocks in Scotland.

Lightning Source UK Ltd.
Milton Keynes UK
UKRC01n1404141116
287536UK00001BA/1